RUTH:

Redemption for the Broken

RUTH:

Redemption for the Broken

Jared C. Wilson

STUDY GUIDE WITH LEADER'S NOTES

New
Growth
Press

WWW.NEWGROWTHPRESS.COM

New Growth Press, Greensboro, NC 27404
www.newgrowthpress.com
Copyright © 2019 by Jared C. Wilson

Cover Design: Faceout Books, faceoutstudio.com
Interior Typesetting and eBook: lparnellbookservices.com
Exercises and Application Questions: Jack Klumpenhower

ISBN 978-1-948130-93-6 (Print)
ISBN 978-1-948130-99-8 (eBook)

Printed in the United States of America

26 25 24 23 22 21 20 19   2 3 4 5 6

CONTENTS

INTRODUCTION

About midway through the book of Ruth, Boaz says to Ruth, "A full reward be given you by the LORD, the God of Israel, under whose wings you have come to take refuge!" (Ruth 2:12). That is more than just a summary of what happens in the book. One wonders if that blessing also became a bit of family lore, or a repeated teaching topic around the dinner table, because in five of the psalms attributed to Ruth's great-grandson David, he wrote and sang and prayed about how God's wings are our refuge (see Psalms 17:8; 36:7; 57:1; 61:4; 63:7).

You see, Ruth is about God's care in the midst of life's disappointments, but it is also a story about family. There's a legacy in this book, and an inheritance. There are reminders of God's goodness in generations past, echoes of a Brother who sacrificed everything to redeem the entire clan, and hints of a family feast still to be celebrated. Amid the struggles of life here and now, there is good news of God's enduring bounty.

And if you belong to Jesus by faith, Ruth is *your* family story. It is your spiritual heritage, more personal and true and lasting than if you had discovered an old scrapbook in your grandmother's attic. So gather with some other members of God's family and open the pages together. Reminisce and imagine. Learn from your common history and shared future how to trust your Father today.

HOW TO USE THIS STUDY

Like the other small group resources in this series, *Ruth: Redemption for the Broken* has a distinct focus. Your goal will be bigger than merely to study the book of Ruth. You will also be learning to keep your eyes on Jesus, the ultimate Redeemer behind the redeemer in the story. And you will consider how the fullness of his love for you takes you beyond yourself, to love others—including those who are poor or are outsiders like Ruth.

This guide will help you do this in a group study. Studying with others in your spiritual family lets you benefit from what God is also teaching them, and it gives you encouragement as you apply what you learn.

Gospel-centered growth includes growing in awareness of your sin and in confidence that Jesus saves you in every way from that sin. Therefore, the group will be a place to share not only successes, but also sins and needs. Expect differences in how people participate. It's okay if some in the group are cheery while others are weary, if some "get it" quickly while others want to look more deeply, or if some are eager to share while others take it slowly. But because you'll be studying the Bible and praying together, also expect God's Spirit to work and change people—starting with you!

Each participant should have one of these study guides in order to join in reading and be able to work through the exercises during that part of the study. The study leader should read through both the lesson and the leader's notes in the back of this book before each lesson begins. Otherwise, no preparation or homework is required from any participant.

There are eight lessons in this study guide. Each lesson will take about an hour to complete, perhaps a bit more if your group is large. The lessons include these elements:

BIG IDEA. This is a summary of the main point of the lesson.

BIBLE CONVERSATION. You will read a passage from the Bible and discuss it. As the heading suggests, the Bible conversation questions are intended to spark a conversation rather than generate correct answers. In most cases, the questions will have several possible good answers and a few best answers. The leader's notes at the back of this book provide some insights, but don't just turn there for the "right answer." At times you may want to see what the notes say, but always try to answer for yourself first by thinking about the Bible passage.

ARTICLE. This is the main teaching section of the lesson, written by the book's author.

DISCUSSION. The discussion questions following the article will help you apply the teaching to your life. Again, there will be several good ways to answer each question.

EXERCISE. The exercise is a section you will complete on your own during group time. You can write in the book if that helps you, or you can just think about your responses. You will then share some of what you learned with the group. If the group is large, it may help to split up to share the results of the exercise and to pray, so that everyone has a better opportunity to participate.

WRAP-UP AND PRAYER. Prayer is a critical part of the lesson because your spiritual growth will happen through God's work in you, not by your self-effort. You will be asking him to do that good work.

The book of Ruth will show you what a sure refuge you have in Jesus. Whatever your disappointments in life or wherever you have doubts, you will see his concern and his eagerness to welcome you. You will hear him once again tell you the gospel—the family story you share with him.

1

EVERYTHING FALLS APART

BIG IDEA

Bitter experiences provoke many different feelings about God. One response is to cling to him, knowing that he also clings to us.

BIBLE CONVERSATION *20 minutes*

Before we begin reading the book of Ruth, let's get familiar with the time and places it mentions:

- *The days when the judges ruled* was an early period in Israel's history, more than a thousand years before the birth of Jesus. The people suffered from weak leadership, so that "everyone did what was right in his own eyes" (Judges 21:25).
- *Judah* was one of Israel's largest tribes, living in the southern region. Prophecy said Judah would rule the rest of Israel (see Genesis 49:8–10), but no king had yet emerged.

- *Bethlehem* was a town of Judah. Its name means "house of bread," but it was experiencing famine. You're probably familiar with another Bethlehem-based Bible story, which Ruth will eventually hint at.
- *Moab* was a neighboring and ungodly land. Its people were considered "unclean," and came from a line begun through incest (see Genesis 19:30–37). Marrying them was ill-advised, since they worshiped false gods and were forbidden from joining in worship of the true God due to past sins (see Deuteronomy 23:3).

Now have a few group members take turns reading **Ruth 1:1–14** aloud. Then discuss the questions below.

List several problems Naomi faces or worries she might have. Which would most worry you if you were in her situation?

If you were assigning blame for all that happened to Naomi's family, whom might you say was responsible, and why? Consider several possibilities.

What difference might it make who Naomi feels is responsible for her troubles? How might it change what Naomi and Ruth do as their lives go forward?

Notice Naomi's beliefs and feelings about God. Do any of them seem either wrong or admirable, and why? Which of these beliefs and feelings about God has been part of your own life? Explain.

****

Now read the following article from this book's author. Have participants read it aloud, taking turns at the paragraph breaks.

Lesson

ARTICLE

Hanging On for Dear Life

5 minutes

This is a love story. But probably not the way you think of love stories. Yes, it has a man, a woman, a matchmaker, and a wedding, but this is not some cutesy, romantic movie script. In the four short chapters of the biblical book of Ruth we have a complex interweaving of family history, socioeconomic commentary, racial and religious culture, and of course depths (and shallows) of human desires and longing. Yes, there is a romance here, but there is actually more than one in this book, and the central, most important romance of all remains implicit.

But we are getting ahead of ourselves. First, we are introduced to the family when it all fell apart. One unique thing about the book of Ruth is its setting within the larger narrative of Old Testament history. This little story is backdropped by the story found in the previous book, Judges. It may be good to take another look through that book if you are not familiar with it, because the world of Judges is full of sin-sick depravity and violence.

It's against that setting filled with blood and perversion that we get this little love story called Ruth. And the beginning could not look bleaker. Ruth's father-in-law Elimelech had originally moved his wife and sons from Israel into the land of Moab in order to improve their lot due to a famine in their home country. The original plan was likely to sojourn until such time as they could return home, but they ended up staying there, and Elimelech's sons took Moabite wives. The Moabites generally worshiped a god called Chemosh, making them pagan people the Jews weren't supposed to marry.

But these good Jewish boys married them anyway. And then Elimelech died. And then the boys died. So the story starts in a fairly rough fashion, the widowed Naomi and her two pagan daughters-in-law, also widows, trying to figure out what to do.

It should not be too difficult to apply this scenario to some moment in our own lives. You may not have lost a spouse or a roof over your head, but it's quite likely if you've lived long enough that you have felt so overwhelmed by the circumstances in your life that you have no idea what to do next. Every option seems to offer little prospect of hope. Every step you take is in the weakness of faith rather than the confidence of sight.

Naomi decides to go home, mainly because she has heard the Lord has been gracious to end the famine there. But it is not as though she is returning as a woman of joy and means. This decision is merely the least bad option before her. Yet there's something Naomi is doing we can all learn from. She does not give up her belief that the Lord is at work, and his plan is good. How do we know this?

Well, first of all, she loves her foreigner daughters-in-law. As filled with bitterness as she is, Naomi loves these women and wants what is best for them. When she tells them to return to their mothers' homes, she's not trying to get rid of them. She is trusting that the Lord will deal kindly with them in the place of their own people. Naomi knows that they are grief-stricken too, but also that they are more likely to find new husbands in the land of their ancestors.

The scene of their imminent parting is quite moving. "Then she kissed them, and they lifted up their voices and wept." Make no mistake: parting with her daughters-in-law is part of Naomi's bitterness. Given how much she obviously has come to love them and how kind they have been to her, she would prefer to keep them with her rather than journey alone as an older woman back to Judah. But she puts others before herself, and thus affirms the sovereignty of God over the situation.

We also know that Naomi, despite her fear and grief, is trusting in the Lord because she ultimately ascribes all her troubles to his sovereign hand! "The hand of the LORD has gone out against me," she says. In her own way, she is echoing the pledge of allegiance of the most famous biblical sufferer: "The LORD gave, and the LORD has taken away; blessed be the name of the LORD" (Job 1:21). Naomi knows that whatever happens next—whether good or bad—like everything that has come before, it must pass through the sovereign control of the one true God.

And then a curious thing happens. Orpah returns Naomi's farewell kiss. She says goodbye. But Ruth latches on. The Hebrew word that is translated "clung to her" in verse 14 is *davaq*, the same word used in Genesis to describe the marriage covenant of man and wife cleaving to one another.

Now, keep in mind, as Iain Duguid says, Ruth "would be about as welcome in Bethlehem as a ham sandwich at a bar mitzvah."[1] But despite all the odds against being happy, finding a husband, and being welcome in the land of God's people, Ruth tells Naomi she is with her, no matter what.

Isn't this a wonderful picture of faith for you and me? Ruth had certainly learned a few things from her believing mother-in-law, bitter or not. Namely, she learned that when you convert to the one true God, you don't throw in the towel when things get difficult. Despite all the odds, she says to Naomi, "I'm with you. I'm going 'all in' with you."

Naomi and Ruth had abandoned themselves to God, and because of that, they were willing to commit themselves to each other's blessing. When everything falls apart, you can trust the God who holds everything together.

And the biggest reason we can do this is because he has done it for us. When Christ the Lord gave up all he'd known to inhabit the land of the foreigner, he surrendered to the will of the Father, despite the bitterest prospect of all—the cross. And yet he went. To honor the good plan of God. And to bless "pagan" outsiders like us. When everything falls part, cling to him for dear life. For he is clinging to you, and not even death will part you.

DISCUSSION *15 minutes*

(NOTE: This opening lesson's discussion is meant to help your group get to know each other by talking about experiences with God. It is common—and perfectly okay—for these experiences to vary greatly from person to person because God's methods

---

1. Iain M. Duguid, *Esther and Ruth* (Phillipsburg, NJ: P & R Publishing, 2005), 142.

and progress are different in each of us. It's also normal for some people to be more eager than others to talk about their experiences with God. So take the pressure off yourself: feel free to share whatever you like, as much or little as you like.)

What hardships or troubles have you had, or when have you felt overwhelmed by circumstances? If you've ever felt bitter or resigned to unhappiness, you might tell about that.

How have your hard times affected the way you think about God, or how you interact with him? For example, you may have done some of the following:

blamed God

ignored God

decided God doesn't help

prayed to God

questioned God

found God for the first time

learned something about God or about yourself

felt/done something else

Naomi gave her daughters-in-law a choice: stay in Moab and have husbands, children and respect, or come to Bethlehem and have nothing except God. When have you faced similar decision points about God, and what was that experience like?

EXERCISE

In God's Hands

15 minutes

In this exercise, you will use a specific example to consider what it might look like in your life for you to know that God clings to you, and for you to cling to him as well. First work through the three steps on your own. Try to reach an answer in each section, writing them down if that is helpful. When everyone is finished, you will have an opportunity to share some of your insights.

STEP 1: BITTERNESS IN LIFE. Pick a hardship or concern in your life that you are willing to think through and talk about. It may be past, present, or a future situation you're worried about.

A problem, concern, or source of bitterness in my life is/was:

_____

_____ .

STEP 2: GOD CLINGS TO YOU. Consider how God clings to you even when he brings bitter situations. Pick a Bible passage that encourages you to see how you are in God's hands, and tell why you find that passage helpful.

> I give them eternal life, and they will never perish, and no one will snatch them out of my hand. My Father, who has given them to me, is greater than all, and no one is able to snatch them out of the Father's hand. (John 10:28–29)

> For I am sure that neither death nor life, nor angels nor rulers, nor things present nor things to come, nor powers, nor height nor depth, nor anything else in all creation, will be able to separate us from the love of God in Christ Jesus our Lord. (Romans 8:38–39)

> Where shall I go from your Spirit?
>   Or where shall I flee from your presence?
> If I ascend to heaven, you are there!
>   If I make my bed in Sheol, you are there!
> If I take the wings of the morning
>   and dwell in the uttermost parts of the sea,
> even there your hand shall lead me,
>   and your right hand shall hold me. (Psalm 139:7–10)

> According to his great mercy, he has caused us to be born again to a living hope through the resurrection of Jesus Christ from the dead, to an inheritance that is imperishable, undefiled, and unfading, kept in heaven for you, who by God's power are being guarded through faith for a salvation ready to be revealed in the last time. In this you rejoice, though now for a little while, if necessary, you have been grieved by various trials. (1 Peter 1:3–6)

Other Bible passage: _____ .
When life gets bitter, this passage can encourage
me because

_____

_____ .

STEP 3: YOU CLING TO GOD. Knowing that God clings to
you, think about how you might be encouraged to cling to him.
Pick at least one response and complete it.

Like Naomi, I can believe that God remains in charge
even when life is bitter. One way I can rely on his care is

_____

_____ .

Like Naomi, I can entrust family members and other
loved ones to God's care. A way I might do this is

_____

_____ .

Like Naomi, I can move toward life with God's people
instead of hiding away in my own country. One way to
do this is

_____

_____ .

Like Naomi, I can be honest with God about my feelings and frustrations. One way I can draw personally closer to him is

_____

_____ .

Now share some of your observations and desires with the group. If God has been helping you grow in these things, tell about that. (NOTE: When someone else is sharing, you can probably be helpful to them too—by listening rather than offering advice.)

WRAP-UP AND PRAYER *5 minutes*

Take time to thank God for what he's done in the lives of your group and to ask him to continue his good work. Pray especially that God would help you cling to him in any ways you've mentioned. Spending time in prayer is a way to practice trusting God and to remember that even our progress in faith is ultimately *his* work. Because of this, we will continually turn to God in prayer during the course of this study.

Lesson

2

THE BLESSING
IN THE BITTER END

BIG IDEA

Faith means giving up everything else for Jesus, a choice made possible by his unwavering faithfulness to us.

BIBLE CONVERSATION *20 minutes*

Where our story left off, Naomi was returning to Bethlehem after about ten years in the pagan land of Moab, where her husband and both of her sons died. One of her Moabite daughters-in-law, Ruth, clung to her despite the fact that a life in Israel, where the true God was worshiped, appeared to offer few prospects for a young woman from Moab. Pick up the story by having someone read **Ruth 1:15–22** aloud. Then discuss the questions that follow.

What are some good ways to describe Ruth's resolve to stay with Naomi? How does it compare to commitments you have made to people?

What might you conclude about Ruth based on her pledge to Naomi? Look closely at Ruth's words, and speculate about her character, her deepest motivations, her knowledge of God, and more.

Once the pair arrives in Bethlehem, Naomi (whose name means "pleasant") repeats her sad story by telling people to call her a name that means "bitter." Do you find it refreshing that she's open about her frustrations with God, or are you tired of her complaints? Explain why.

What evidence is there already that God may be blessing Naomi, even if she can't see it yet?

✳✳✳✳

Now read the article, "For Better or for Worse," aloud, taking turns at the paragraph breaks. Then discuss the questions at the end of the article.

Lesson

ARTICLE

For Better or for Worse

5 minutes

Often the children of God are only able to step forward in faith after they've properly considered the alternatives, especially if faith will mean uncertain outcomes or even outcomes they know for certain will be difficult. For Ruth, Naomi may have made a good case that parting ways was for the best. Ruth could stay with her people, and her prospects for acceptance and maybe even marriage would be much higher. To enter into Israel would be to expose herself to all the hardships of being a childless widow and a Moabite, in a place where the cultural and ethnic chips were stacked against her.

But the alternative was no alternative at all for Ruth. As a follower of the Lord, she preferred an unfamiliar land that honored him to a familiar place dominated by idolatry. And she preferred enduring hardship with the mother-in-law she was committed to rather than remaining with her kinsmen alone.

As we saw in the previous passage, this commitment Ruth makes to Naomi is a grace-driven kind of covenant—born of real, selfless love with God at the center—and now she even makes a kind of vow: "Do not urge me to leave you or to return from following you. For where you go I will go, and where you lodge I will lodge. Your people shall be my people, and your God my God. Where you die I will die, and there will I be buried. May the LORD do so to me and more also if anything but death parts me from you" (vv. 16–17).

One of the more surprising and fascinating aspects of this vow is Ruth's commitment *beyond* Naomi—"Where you die I will die, and there will I be buried." In a wedding vow, for instance, we commit "till death do us part." When a spouse dies, most of us recognize that the widow or widower is free. The covenant is no longer binding because one of the parties is no longer alive. What Ruth is doing is demonstrating more than a great loyalty to Naomi. She has not put on Jewishness just to go along to get along. She really is a worshiper of God. Note that she knows and uses his personal name in verse 17—the Hebrew letters *YHWH*, which are written as "LORD" in most of our Bibles.

Ruth really is committing to Naomi's faith and to her people, regardless of what it means for her—so much so that when Naomi dies, Ruth isn't bailing. She isn't going back to Moab. Ever.

And here we see our first big clue that the love story of Ruth is bigger than her relationship with Boaz (who isn't even on the scene yet). And it's even bigger than the familial love and spiritual bond Ruth has made to her mother-in-law as part of her relationship with God. That's the first "love story" in the narrative. But the real love story behind and beneath the other love stories in Ruth is the one about God and his people.

In a way, Ruth's commitment is a picture of the faith you and I show whenever we follow Jesus. We don't always know where he will take us. We only know that being with him is better than the alternative. Think of the time in John 6 where Jesus has miraculously fed the five thousand. At the end, by the time he's come to the preaching, the crowd has become offended and has left. They liked the feast; they did not like the faith. So near the end of that scene, Jesus turns to his closest disciples, who have now seen vividly how unpopular Jesus can be when he gets to the point of demanding discipleship. He asks, "Do you guys want to leave too?" and Peter wisely says, "Where would we go?"

Peter, in that moment at least, has come to see the alternatives as no alternative at all. Only Christ has the word of life. So even if he leads us through the valley of the shadow of death, we can fear no evil because he's with us. This is a ripple effect of Ruth's faith, as we will see later in the book.

But in a much truer and much better way, Ruth's commitment is a picture of the commitment Jesus himself makes to *us*. Like us, Ruth is imperfect; she is a sinner and thus prone to wander. But the sinless Christ has made his vow to us no matter what.

Even in the face of our sin, Jesus doesn't blink. Nothing surprises him. Nothing fazes him. Not even the prospect of being loved back imperfectly or infrequently will send him packing. Our well-meaning friends may decide the prospect of our pain and junk spilling into their lives isn't worth it. They see our habits and our baggage and our self-interested patterns and they wish us well, but sadly, like Orpah, choose another path. But not our friend Jesus! He sets his face toward the cross, scorning its shame, and makes his covenant with us to the bitter end.

Jesus, like Ruth, makes his commitment to the ones he loves for better or worse. But unlike Ruth, he knows just how bad the "worse" is going to be. Still he stays.

Ruth stays too, and things do not look great for her in the immediate wake of her commitment. She and her bitter mother-in-law make the journey to Bethlehem. It is hard to see the wisdom in Ruth's decision. They are poor. They are widows. She is a Moabite. Her mother-in-law is really kind of a downer. I wonder if Ruth ever had second thoughts.

But she went. Why? Because her vow had been made. It had been made out of love for God and love for Naomi. Ruth was willing to venture into the unknown because her love was greater than her fear.

I think of Jesus in that garden mere minutes before his betrayal and arrest, mere hours before his torture and crucifixion. The agony of the cross is already gripping his flesh. In his prayers he is sweating blood. In the near distance, his friends nap. He is doing this for *them*?

Yes, and for us. Jesus even prayed for you in that garden. Did you know that? John 17:20 says he prayed for all who *will* believe because of the apostles' message in the future. "The world will know that you sent me and have loved them even as you have loved me" (v. 23).

Christ's vow has been made. It has been made out of love for the Father and love for you. Jesus was willing to venture even to death on a cross because his love was greater than his fear. And because his love is greater than your sin.

DISCUSSION *10 minutes*

What aspect of Ruth's faith most impresses you? How would you like your own faith to be more like hers? Explain how your life might look different with that kind of faith.

If it were truer of you that you "fear no evil" because God is with you, where might you dare to go? How would it free you up to care for others in new ways?

Lesson

EXERCISE

Losses and Gains

15 minutes

Jesus gave a bit of teaching that may remind you of Ruth. He said, "Everyone who has left houses or brothers or sisters or father or mother or children or lands, for my name's sake, will receive a hundredfold and will inherit eternal life" (Matthew 19:29). This gospel call from Jesus contains two parts: (1) you are prepared to lose everything you have (2) to gain Jesus and all he offers.

For this exercise, read through the chart below. It lists things you may have given up for Jesus and things you have gained in him. Decide which items are especially true of your life or meaningful to you. You might circle some items or make a few notes in the margins to explain. When everyone is ready, discuss the questions at the end of the exercise together.

To follow Jesus, I have lost/given up...	By following Jesus, I have gained...
A worldly possession: _____	An eternal inheritance that shall last, kept in heaven for me (1 Peter 1:4)
Support of family or friends	The deep unity, sympathy, love, and tenderness of the family of God (1 Peter 3:8)
A romantic or other relationship that didn't honor God	The steadfast love of God, which he will never remove even though I sin (Psalm 89:33)
Approval of friends or superiors, or fame and acclaim	The approval of God and the gladness of all creation when I am revealed as his child (Romans 8:19)
An opportunity in my career, school, or community: _____	The satisfaction and honor of working for Christ's everlasting kingdom (Daniel 7:14)
A sinful habit that displeased my heavenly Father: _____	The joyful habit of loving what is true, honorable, just, pure, lovely, commendable, excellent, and praiseworthy (Philippians 4:8)
A selfish priority that came before concern for others: _____	The grace to grow in compassion, kindness, humility, meekness, and patience (Colossians 3:12)
The urge to live up to standards set by others or myself	The forgiveness of sin and righteousness from God that comes through my faith in Christ (Philippians 3:9)

Which items especially seem to fit your life or strike you as particularly meaningful? Explain why.

If you had a hard time thinking of many things you've given up to follow Jesus, consider the possibility that you've not fully faced up to his call to come to him only, the way Ruth had to. What might Jesus still be calling you to give up so that the blessings you have in him become your whole life?

If you had a hard time feeling thrilled by what you have gained in Jesus, consider the possibility that your joy in the gospel should grow. Which of these blessings would you like God to make more precious to you, and why? How would it help you care for others?

WRAP-UP AND PRAYER *10 minutes*

Pray together that God would help you loosen your grip on things of this world and see his beauty instead. Pray that he would lessen your fears and make you more willing to care for others. Pray that you would know more of his unfailing devotion to you.

3

THINGS TAKE A TURN

BIG IDEA

Ruth and Boaz show us the difference between true faith and self-trust, and between true godliness and self-interest.

BIBLE CONVERSATION *20 minutes*

Today's passage in Ruth speaks of gleaning. In ancient Israel God's law provided for the poorest of the poor to eke out a meager existence by gleaning in the grain fields. Harvesters were supposed to ignore scattered parts of the crop that would hardly be worth the effort anyway—like solitary stalks at the edges of the field or those accidentally dropped—and leave them for gleaners to gather. Gleaning was hard work with little reward, and harvesters didn't always take kindly to gleaners, but it was a way to stay alive.

Now have someone read **Ruth 2:1–13** aloud. Then discuss the following questions:

This passage introduces Boaz. Look closely at his interactions when he arrives at the workplace he owns. What does he ask about and see to? What can you conclude about his character or his managerial style?

What does Boaz admire about Ruth? Among men you know, how common is his way of thinking?

Other parts of the Bible tell us that Boaz's ancestors included Rahab, another pagan outsider who believed in the true God and was brought into the Israelite community (see Joshua 6:25 and Matthew 1:5). What might Boaz have understood about God, and outsiders, that other Israelites missed?

In his blessing to Ruth, Boaz says, "The LORD repay you for what you have done, and a full reward be given you by the LORD, the God of Israel, under whose wings you have come to take refuge!" (v. 12). How would this blessing encourage you if someone spoke it to you?

* * * *

Read the following article aloud, taking turns at the paragraph breaks, and then discuss the questions.

Love at First Sight

5 minutes

This is the part of the story where the guy meets the girl. But if you read the passage carefully, you will see this is not nearly the same kind of "meet-cute" we see in Hollywood productions. In your typical romantic movie, our featured couple runs into each other in some happenstance way, exchanges witty but superficial banter, and somehow in the midst of this flirting falls madly in love.

We all know real life doesn't work that way. We also know, especially if we've been married for a while, that the best kind of romance actually doesn't kick in until things get deep, even difficult. Witty and flirty are fun, but they are not the stuff of covenantal commitment.

And yet, the way Ruth and Boaz meet doesn't look much like real life either. This is not because it didn't happen or isn't realistic. It's simply because the faith and the righteousness they both display here is so exceptional. It's no wonder the Lord wanted it recorded as Scripture, and it's no wonder he orchestrated this particular romance as a vital plot point in his epic plan of redemption.

The first notable thing we see here about Ruth is how she found favor with a godly, potential husband. She did it by being godly herself. She humbly acknowledged her poverty, resolved to provide for Naomi, and worked hard at the unpleasant chore this required. She didn't go strutting around the field, inquiring about Boaz and his likes and dislikes. She, in effect, prayerfully minded her own business. Her work ethic was her witness. If any man was going to take a shine to her, it must really be *her*, not some image she was projecting.

Well, that's different.

Like the rest of the poor gleaners, Ruth takes up residence in the margins of the field, picking up scraps. Then Boaz shows up. And of all the ordinary men in the Bible we regard as heroes, Boaz is likely the one guy who actually deserves it. Abraham, Moses, David, and the others—they all have their moments of dirtbaggery. But Boaz, though we don't see all that much about him in the biblical record, comes across as *Pride & Prejudice*'s Mr. Darcy crossed with *Sense & Sensibility*'s Colonel Brandon. And while I know I'm mixing my Austenian noblemen here, the takeaway is that every woman ought to want a Boaz and every parent of daughters should hope they find one.

Our first clue is that his workers call out to bless him as he comes walking by. Our next clue is how he first responds to the sight of Ruth. "Whose young woman is this?" he asks. He doesn't say who is she? Instead he asks *whose* is she? In other words, his inquiry has concern for her protection and belonging already embedded in it. His use of *daughter* in verse 8 also doesn't just indicate an age difference, but the kind of care he already wants Ruth to know. And verse 1 has told us that Boaz is a "worthy" man, referring to a variety of attributes—valor, wealth, moral character. Boaz was, in other words, the total package.

Here the gospel application shifts for us. When we looked at Ruth in chapter 1, we saw in her traces of Christological typology (meaning she was a pattern for Christ who would come later). But now we see that pattern mostly in Boaz; it is he who is like Jesus. And when we notice that in this text, we also find a valuable application in Ruth's first encounter with him.

"Then she fell on her face, bowing to the ground, and said to him, 'Why have I found favor in your eyes, that you should take notice of me, since I am a foreigner?'" (verse 10). We know Ruth is brimming with faith because, after all her hard work, she still wonders at Boaz's taking notice of her. This is not only a right attitude toward him, but more importantly a right attitude toward God.

These are important dynamics to get straight in the Christian life: the relationship between faith and works and the distinction between gospel and law. If we do not keep them straight, even if close together, we end up thinking screwy thoughts and doing screwy things.

Self-righteousness is so insidious, so subtle. We hardly know when we're engaging in it, if only because it is every sinner's default state. So many times as we seek to follow Christ, we wind up adopting some shallow, performance-based version of the gospel in which we expect that our hard work is earning some kind of credit, whether material or spiritual, with God. It is deceptively easy for us to think to ourselves, *Well, of course God will notice me. I'm working hard for him. I deserve this favor.*

And when we do that, we lose the awe we ought to experience over his grace.

For all her industriousness and diligent faithfulness, Ruth stood in awe that Boaz would notice her. Her humility is a sterling example to us all of how to stay low before God.

Here we see real love at first sight. It's not romance the way a greeting card presents it. There are no rainbows and butterflies. There is only a man concerned about the well-being and protection of a woman and a woman honoring the dignity and favor of a man. Unlike the typical love at first sight in the movies, we might be able to actually work with this kind of love! This is the start of real love, where each heart is set on the good and dignity of the other.

Even when Boaz praises her faithfulness at the end of our passage, Ruth's interest is still in how he shows favor to her despite her foreignness. She seems surprised that he would take notice of her in the first place. She certainly seems surprised that he would in some way want to bless her. Ruth is amazed by grace.

Did you know that God isn't looking for employees? It's not like he needs the help. Yes, we obey God, and yes, we serve him as subjects in the conquering kingdom of Christ. But Christ's yoke is easy and his burden is light. And being united to Christ by faith is not so tenuous as to be dependent on our religious output. "No longer do I call you servants . . ." Jesus says to his disciples, "but I have called you friends" (John 15:15).

Stay low. Stay humble. Stay faithful. But know that the good news means that the Lord's favor on you is not dependent on you! It's neither started nor sustained by your hard work. His grace for you is really grace! It comes out of the overflow of his love, out of his care and concern, out of the very fact that Jesus Christ is the most "worthy man" who ever existed, and that in fact, before you ever existed to work or not work, the preexistent Son of God determined that you'd be noticed, rewarded, and hidden under his wings.

DISCUSSION *10 minutes*

What insights into godly behavior have you noticed by reading about Boaz and Ruth? How would you like to become more like them?

The article mentioned that Jesus does not have employees who must constantly prove their religious output. Rather, he has disciples he loves and even calls friends. How might this truth encourage you to be more like Boaz and Ruth?

Lesson

EXERCISE

Receiving and Giving Grace

15 minutes

The Bible tells us that if we have come to Jesus by faith, our story is much like Ruth's. We too were outsiders, part of a people hostile to God. But Jesus died for us to bring us into his family, by grace.

> Remember that you were at that time separated from Christ, alienated from the commonwealth of Israel and strangers to the covenants of promise, having no hope and without God in the world. But now in Christ Jesus you who once were far off have been brought near by the blood of Christ. For he himself is our peace, who has made us both one and has broken down in his flesh the dividing wall of hostility. (Ephesians 2:12–14)

Clearly, this means Ruth is a model for us. But so is Boaz. Ruth is a model in *receiving* grace, while Boaz is a model in *giving* grace. Once we become believers, both receiving and giving grace are habits of an ongoing Christian life.

For this exercise, look through the list of habits of a receiving-grace lifestyle and a giving-grace lifestyle. Note some habits that God seems to have brought into your life—or some you hope he will grow in you. Then discuss the questions together.

A LIFESTYLE OF *RECEIVING* GRACE

I am **thankful**. Like Ruth, I know I have no reason to expect kindness, so I am constantly grateful for all Jesus did for me when I was one of the outsiders.

I am **teachable**. I am willing to have God and others point out my faults and needs, and I receive correction humbly rather than defensively.

I am **sin-aware**. I look beyond surface sins that are easy to admit and confess the sin in my heart, which I can't eradicate on my own.

I am **listening**. I crave God's Word, submitting to both its discipline and its encouragement as I regularly read it and hear it preached.

I am **prayerful**. I daily ask God for the grace I need and for more closeness with him, desiring him to get the glory for all my progress, and realizing as I grow that I need to pray even more.

I am **connected**. I stay close to other believers for support and correction, allowing them to poke around in my life.

I am **Christ-leaning**. Rather than trying first to solve problems on my own, or to resist sin on my own, or to please God on my own, I seek Jesus's help from the start.

I am **Spirit-reliant**. My work to be godly is not a performance *for* God, but a joint effort *with* God.

Other: _____

_____

_____

A LIFESTYLE OF *GIVING* GRACE

I am **generous**. Like Boaz, I share with those in need and have compassion for the poor.

I am **welcoming**. I go out of my way to help foreigners or cultural outsiders feel at home and thrive in my community, church, and family.

I am **inclusive**. I look for social outsiders, lonely people, or those who aren't much fun, and I befriend them even if it costs me status with the in-crowd.

I am **evangelistic**. I get excited about sharing the gospel with people who haven't heard much about Jesus, or with religious outsiders whom others write off as uninterested or consider "bad guys."

I am **kind**. I show love, not contempt, toward unbelievers or those who are theologically wrong, even when they oppose me.

I am **intercessory**. I pray for others, including those who persecute me.

I am **Christ-pointing**. I seldom miss an opportunity to point others to Jesus, being more concerned that they see how he is right and good than that they think I am right and good.

I am **sacrificial**. My concern for others extends far enough that I give up my own comforts, possessions, time, and dignity.

Other: _____

_____

_____

Share some of your observations with the group. Which habits do you see in yourself? Which do hope to see more of, and why?

How do you see the two lists being connected in your life? For example, how might stronger habits of receiving grace help you give grace? Or how might the challenges of giving grace reveal your own need to receive grace? Try to give examples.

WRAP-UP AND PRAYER *10 minutes*

Since both receiving and giving grace are unnatural to our sinful selves, living the way the exercise describes is hard. We can easily feel condemned by our poor showing or discouraged that this sort of life is impossible. The solution is to turn to God.

- *Instead of feeling condemned*, trust Jesus and how he lived this way on your behalf and died for you to give you his righteousness.

Lesson 3: Things Take a Turn 39

- *Instead of feeling incapable,* rely on the Holy Spirit's power in you to make you more like Jesus. Ask him to work in you.

Make these expressions of faith the focus of your closing prayer time together.

Lesson

4

THINGS ARE LOOKING UP

BIG IDEA

God's love for us in Christ is radically inclusive, radically extravagant, radically glorious, and radically transforming.

BIBLE CONVERSATION *20 minutes*

When we left off, Ruth was gleaning in Boaz's fields. Gleaners could hope to take home a meager amount of grain at the end of a day, barely enough to live on. Paid harvesters, in contrast, might be given a liter or so of grain for their work—enough to support a family. Today's passage also mentions a large amount called an *ephah*, equivalent to roughly twenty liters or thirty pounds in weight.

Have someone read **Ruth 2:14–23** aloud. Then discuss the questions below.

In this passage, Ruth experiences a change-your-life day. How does her life appear to be changing, and what must she be feeling at lunchtime?

In the afternoon?
At the end of the workday?
After returning to Naomi?

If you were Ruth thinking back on your day at bedtime, what would be your most lasting impression, and why would it be particularly meaningful to you?

Naomi sums up the message of this passage when she says the Lord's "kindness has not forsaken the living or the dead!" (v. 20). How is the kindness Boaz displayed like the kindness of God? List several ways, and tell which is especially encouraging to you.

****

Now read this lesson's article, "Close By to the End." Read it aloud, taking turns at the paragraph breaks.

Close By to the End

5 minutes

It is amazing how grace can change one's disposition even if it has not changed one's immediate circumstances. Bitter Naomi has found some joy by the end of chapter 2, and it is the culmination of a succession of four portraits of grace.

The first portrait we see is the **radical inclusion of the gospel**. That Boaz invites Ruth to his table to partake of bread and wine with him is astonishing. It is a shocking scene because she is a single woman and he is a man, because she is poor and he is rich, because she is a woman of Moab and he is an Israelite.

I think of all the blessed trouble Jesus stirred up consorting with all the wrong people—lepers and tax collectors and women of ill repute. Nobody who ever confronted him about this seemed to consider that they didn't belong at his table either. The twelve disciples around that table in the upper room, by all fleshly reckoning, did not belong there. And yet Jesus shared his bread and wine with them. Just as he does with us.

The only people this doesn't impress are those who think themselves impressive. Boaz owes Ruth nothing. Neither does Christ owe us a single thing. Boaz doesn't even wait for Ruth to become impressive. He knows she can't. Similarly, Jesus died for us while we were sinners. He's not waiting for us to get worthy of his grace. Grace is called grace because it is for the unworthy!

The second portrait of grace is the **radical extravagance of the gospel**. Ruth ate until she was satisfied. Boaz does not relegate her to the scraps. He brings her to the table and lets her get full. And when she returns to Naomi, it is with enough for both of them to eat for weeks. Boaz is extravagant in how much grain he allows Ruth to gather. In fact, when she returns to Naomi after just the first day, Ruth has as much grain as a hired worker would earn for two weeks of solid labor. Starvation is no longer going to be a possibility for them now that Boaz has extended God's grace to them.

Similarly, the Lord's provision is no mere pittance. He is not stingy with his gifts. If you drink of the water he gives, you will never be thirsty. If you eat the bread of his flesh and the wine of his blood, you will never die. And as Ruth was thereafter inclined to stick close to Boaz, how could we do better than to stick close to our abundant Provider? As John Calvin said, "In short, since rich store of every kind of good abounds in him, let us drink our fill from this fountain, and from no other."[2]

The third portrait of grace in the passage is in the **radical glory of the gospel**. By law, Ruth was allowed only to glean along the outskirts of the field, picking up the scraps and leftovers. Boaz, however, allows her into the middle of the field with his

---

2. John Calvin, *Institutes of the Christian Religion*, trans. Ford Lewis Battles (Philadelphia: Westminster, 1960), 1:528

employed harvesters. She is given free reign beyond what is required by the law.

The clarifying lens of the New Testament shows just how radiant this really is. Paul writes that as glorious as the law is—because it reflects the very holiness of God—the gospel of God is more glorious still!

> Now if the ministry of death, carved in letters on stone, came with such glory that the Israelites could not gaze at Moses' face because of its glory, which was being brought to an end, will not the ministry of the Spirit have even more glory? For if there was glory in the ministry of condemnation, the ministry of righteousness must far exceed it in glory. Indeed, in this case, what once had glory has come to have no glory at all, because of the glory that surpasses it. For if what was being brought to an end came with glory, much more will what is permanent have glory. (2 Corinthians 3:7–11)

In other words, the law is good but the gospel is better! And the law is glorious, but the gospel of grace is more so. Thus, when Boaz doesn't just fulfill the law but goes beyond it to allow Ruth into the inner folds of the field of harvest, the Lord is providing through him a wonderful picture of the radical glory of the gospel of Jesus.

The fourth and final portrait of grace we see in this passage is in the **radical transformation of the gospel**. In 2 Corinthians 3:18, Paul says that beholding the surpassing glory of Jesus changes us into the likeness of Christ. In a similar way, the provision of Boaz is changing Ruth and Naomi's disposition. This is most seen in Naomi's response to the news of Ruth's favor with Boaz: "May he be blessed by the LORD, whose kindness has not forsaken the living or the dead!"

Naomi thinks her own fortunes may be changing. She's gone from bitter to rejoicing. In the beginning, when her prospects were bleak, she ascribed her difficult lot in life to the sovereignty of God, and here she ascribes the upturn in their personal plot lines to the sovereignty of God. The Lord takes away, but the Lord also gives! Blessed be the name of the Lord!

We also see Ruth's continuing commitment to her new people and her new place. Her "keeping close" to the young women in Boaz's field is an image of this. And the final line of this passage is another: "She lived with her mother-in-law." Ruth is a woman totally transformed by the grace of God. At what point she was converted, we don't exactly know—perhaps in her marriage to her late husband—but we see that her conversion is real. The Moabite lives as an Israelite. Only God could do this.

The commitments Ruth has made are born of the commitments God has made to her. He has redeemed her, made promises to her in the covenants. There is even the prospect, not yet seen, of this poor, pagan widow's place in the history of redemption. She doesn't see that yet, and likely didn't until her vantage point in heavenly glory, but she's trusting the Lord regardless. She is sticking close by all God's blessings as a way of sticking close by him, because through it all, he has condescended to stay close by her.

I don't know if you feel close or far from the Lord. I only know that his commitments to us in the gospel of Jesus are not contingent upon our feelings or circumstances. He is the true friend who sticks closer than a brother. Let's stay close by him, no matter the cost, because he has truly come close by to us. Indeed, by faith, we are hidden with him in the very life of God.

DISCUSSION *10 minutes*

The article said the only people not impressed that Jesus shares his table with them are those who think themselves impressive. How have you found this true, in either the lives of others or your own life?

What is the practical value of humility for a Christian?

How has seeing God's grace changed your disposition? Try to think of a specific way God is good to you (look beyond pleasant circumstances to spiritual blessings as well). How has seeing this made a noticeable change in you?

Gospel Portraits

15 minutes

As we understand the vastness of Jesus's love for us, our love for him and others will grow. This is one practical reason why we want an ever-larger appreciation of the gospel.

For this exercise, think through the four radical portraits of the gospel mentioned in the article. Which of them has become a source of delight to you? How much of a delight, and how often? When everyone is finished, discuss the questions at the end of the article.

I delight in my radical INCLUSION in the gospel:

- I am amazed that Jesus came to seek and to save a stubborn sinner like me, and to bring even me into his family.
- I count it one of my greatest honors that I am invited to eat and drink at Jesus's table when I partake of the Lord's Supper.

- I long for the day when I will feast with Jesus, side by side with other unlikely saints, in the coming kingdom.
- Other: _____ .

_____

O—O—O—O—O—O—O

SELDOM   **OFTEN**

I delight in the radical EXTRAVAGANCE of the gospel:

- I have confidence that my Father will never withhold any good thing from me, so that I would rather spend one day with him than a thousand elsewhere (see Psalm 84:10–11).
- I have joy in how fully God rescues me from sin: I was guilty but now counted righteous, excluded from God but now brought near, selfish but now being made holy, shameful but now honorable, dead but now alive forever, suffering but one day freed.
- I am filled with the expectation of soon seeing "what no eye has seen, nor ear heard, nor the heart of man imagined, what God has prepared for those who love him" (1 Corinthians 2:9).
- Other: _____ .

_____

O—O—O—O—O—O—O

SELDOM   **OFTEN**

I delight in the radical GLORY of the gospel:

- I know of nothing more praiseworthy than that the Son of God would die for a sinner like me and rise again to bring me to glory.
- I abandon the urge for others to see how good, right, and capable I am, preferring the greater glory of sharing in Christ's righteousness and sufferings.
- My great comfort lies in the fact that I don't have to prove myself, but that I belong to my Savior who gloriously proved himself perfectly faithful.
- Other: _____ .

_____

O—O—O—O—O—O—O

SELDOM　　　　　　　　　　　　　**OFTEN**

I delight in my radical TRANSFORMATION in the gospel:

- I consider my best days to be those when God helped me to repent of sin or draw closer to him.
- I am thrilled that God works in me to give me the most elusive freedom: not the freedom to do whatever I want, but the freedom to be the kind of person I should be.
- In my life on earth, I practice with great anticipation for my holy life in heaven.
- Other: _____ .

_____

O—O—O—O—O—O—O

SELDOM　　　　　　　　　　　　　**OFTEN**

Share some of your results with the group. It isn't necessarily bad if you find yourself at the "seldom" end of the scale; it means you can look forward to much more gospel joy as you grow in Christ. Where do you hope to grow in gospel delight, and why?

How might you go about seeking from God more joy in the gospel? Try to be specific about your daily life.

WRAP-UP AND PRAYER *10 minutes*

Begin seeking more joy in the gospel by praying for it. You might also thank God for all he has given you in Christ, or praise him for the glory of the gospel, especially if this lesson brought up blessings you have seldom considered before. Pray also for your process as you seek to receive more gospel joy, that God would help you in it (yes, pray for your praying!).

5

THE PLOT THICKENS

BIG IDEA

The confidence that God is at work in us, and the desire to live for his glory, make bold love possible.

BIBLE CONVERSATION *20 minutes*

Today's passage picks up on the revelation that Ruth and Naomi might have a redeemer, a kinsman willing to buy them back from their destitute situation. By custom, a dead man's relative (usually his brother) might agree to marry the widow, providing for her and also leading to children who would inherit the dead man's property. This could be expensive for the redeemer and it added nothing to his personal estate, so it is no surprise that some men found ways around the responsibility (see Genesis 38:6–11). Ruth's case was that of a Moabite whose most obvious redeemer, her brother-in-law, had also died. So most of Naomi's kinsmen could easily find reasons to turn down the role.

Have someone read **Ruth 3:1–13** aloud. Then discuss the questions below.

RUTH: REDEMPTION FOR THE BROKEN

The situation Naomi orchestrates sounds like one that might lead to sexual sin for some couples. Why does it not lead there for Ruth and Boaz? What is different, and better, about their intentions and desires for each other?

At the very least, Ruth's approach seems rather forward. Why can she dare to be so bold? Think of several reasons.

Ruth's request to Boaz, "Spread your wings over your servant, for you are a redeemer," contains layers of meaning. It recalls Boaz's words about how Ruth sought refuge under God's wings. But the word for *wings* can also mean the edges of a garment or covering, and to spread one's covering over a woman can mean to marry her. It is also used in Ezekiel 16:8 to describe God's caring covenant with his people. With all this in mind, what is Ruth requesting?

Given what you know about Boaz, what might he appreciate about all Ruth asked and how she phrased it?

✶✶✶✶

Now read the article aloud, taking turns at paragraph breaks. Then discuss the questions that follow.

Lesson

ARTICLE

As God Lives

5 minutes

We've now come to the most curious and complex part of the Ruth narrative. Many scholars and teachers have wrestled over just what is taking place in Ruth's initial overture to Boaz as she goes secretly to "uncover his feet" and lie down with him. Some, of course, see something sexually inappropriate taking place here; others do not. Coming to our interpretation humbly is probably a good idea.

One important thing we learn from this nighttime encounter is that, for Ruth and Naomi, faith in God is not a passive, theoretical concept. The God they trust is real, alive, and actively redeeming! Thus, Naomi and Ruth are willing not just to think in faith but to *walk* in faith. This proposal of sorts to Boaz is great evidence of that. The overture may look bold, but that is because bold actions result when faithful people believe in the redemptive purposes of God.

Boaz likewise, being an honorable man of God, is wholehearted about taking part in God's justice and redemption in the world around him. We see this is in the way he conducts his business affairs. We see this in the way he looks after the poor. And we see this in the way he responds to this young woman who has come to him in the dark of night to ask for his covering.

The intentions of both Ruth and Boaz are not to engage in a fling, but in family history! Ruth appeals to Boaz's place in the customary obligation of kinsman redemption. But it looks as though Naomi wasn't as well versed in the family tree as she thought. There's another fellow one place in line ahead of our boy Boaz. Still, his response to his aspiring bride is promising: "Remain tonight, and in the morning, if he will redeem you, good; let him do it. But if he is not willing to redeem you, then, as the LORD lives, I will redeem you. Lie down until the morning" (v. 13).

What is Boaz really saying? First, he is saying his plan to redeem Ruth (and thereby the clan of Elimelech) is as sure as there is a God in heaven. "Will you redeem me?" Ruth asks, and Boaz says (in a way), "As God lives, I will." There is no doubt about it. As surely as God exists, so will Boaz's commitment and obedience.

Second, and more deeply, Boaz is saying that he is going to redeem Ruth *because* God lives. Boaz is the strange sort of man who does things because God exists. In this sense he is the most logical of men. Does God exist? If so, much must be different about my life. I ought to live my life as if God exists.

What if we all applied this standard to our motivations and determinations? What would our lives look like if we really believed the Lord lives? Would it change our outlook on the conflict we find ourselves in? Would it change our perspective on the confusion or anxiety facing us each day? If we knew there was a God who not only ordained these circumstances to come our way but also holds us to a standard of holiness in glorifying him through whatever stage or season of life we must navigate, would it alter our course? Our attitude?

Think of the way Ruth went forward to act on this plan, not putting her own needs first but the needs of Naomi and, by extension, the family honor? She is not simply looking for a hunky guy to marry, but a protector and a leader, one who would not simply help extend the family name, but the name of God.

And think of the way Boaz shows real love for Ruth. He could easily have taken advantage of her. He could have responded to her overtures with cheap promises and the limited pleasures of lust. Instead he demonstrates real love, the kind that looks to the good of the whole person, and the kind of romance that nurtures a whole life together, not a fleeting series of momentary passions.

Ruth and Boaz aren't married just yet, but they are already building their life together upon a reality deeper than sentiment and affection—the reality of God. What if we knew that the God who has appointed us for specific trials or troubles also loves us deeply, affectionately, and irrevocably? How might *that* impact our decision-making?

Deeper still, Boaz is committing to redeem Ruth—to paraphrase C. S. Lewis here—not because a God lives, but because *this* God lives. This means he is going to redeem her in the Lord's way and for the Lord's purposes. LORD is in small caps, denoting the divine name. "As this personal, one true God lives, I will redeem you." According to the LORD's glory, to make that name great, to exalt and glorify the God who is his God, Boaz will do this.

Ruth's redemption is not only or primarily for her glory, nor is it only or primarily for Naomi's or Boaz's or Elimelech's or Mahlon's. It is for God's glory first and foremost that Boaz redeems Ruth. And what glory that turned out to be! Boaz could not have seen it at the time, but his faithful commitment to God's glory would lead not just to a marriage but to a child, and then to a child of that child, and to more children, and finally to the birth of the Messiah himself, Jesus the King who died and rose again to accomplish God's most glorious work of all. But that is a story for a different day.

DISCUSSION *10 minutes*

How would it alter your life to really believe, daily, that the Lord lives and that your actions can bring him glory?

In verse 11, Boaz calls Ruth a "worthy woman." And at the start of chapter 2, Boaz was called a "worthy man." What traits of a worthy man or woman has this story made you want to copy in your life, and why?

5

Doubts and Fears
15 minutes

There was boldness to Ruth's and Boaz's actions and their love, because they believed God was being faithful to them and working through them. When we doubt God is really at work, our fears take over and it's hard to love others.

For this exercise, think about the anxieties and fears that keep you from helping others and loving them boldly. Perhaps you've been scared to go to a faraway place or into a strange situation, or to give help, or to talk about Jesus. Those you fail to love because of your fears might be among the following:

> The poor or others needing help
> Foreigners or people of a different culture
> Friends, coworkers, or neighbors
> People in your church
> People within your own family

Work for a while on your own. Begin by noting some of your more common anxieties that keep you from caring boldly for others.

"I might look foolish."

"I don't know how to start."

"What if it costs more than I can afford?"

"It could get dangerous."

"I'm no good at that. It's better to let someone else do it."

"I could get sucked in further than I want to go."

"It could affect my family (or something else I love)."

"My intentions might be misunderstood."

"There's too much I'm doing already, so I don't have the time/energy."

"They probably don't want someone like me." (fear of rejection)

"My spouse/friends/family wouldn't approve."

"It all sounds too unpredictable."

Other: _____

_____

Next, consider what your anxieties reveal. How do you doubt God's assurances, putting worldly assurances ahead of them? For example, if you marked that you are concerned about getting sucked in too far, and how it all sounds unpredictable, you might conclude: *I place <u>staying in control</u> ahead of believing God's assurances.*

I place _____
ahead of believing God's assurances.

Finally, take a closer look at those assurances of God. Note some that would help you love others more boldly if you stopped doubting and lived as if God really is at work through you.

Godliness is of value in every way, as it holds promise for the present life and also for the life to come. (1 Timothy 4:8)

As for the rich in this present age, charge them not to be haughty, nor to set their hopes on the uncertainty of riches, but on God, who richly provides us with everything to enjoy. They are to do good, to be rich in good works, to be generous and ready to share, thus storing up treasure for themselves as a good foundation for the future, so that they may take hold of that which is truly life. (1 Timothy 6:17–19)

If we love one another, God abides in us and his love is perfected in us. (1 John 4:12)

The LORD will fulfill his purpose for me. (Psalm 138:8)

The Holy Spirit, whom the Father will send in my name, he will teach you all things and bring to your remembrance all that I have said to you. Peace I leave with you; my peace I give to you. Not as the world gives do I give to you. Let not your hearts be troubled, neither let them be afraid. (John 14:26–27)

Yours is the kingdom, O LORD, and you are exalted as head above all. Both riches and honor come from you, and you rule over all. In your hand are power and might, and in your hand it is to make great and to give strength to all. (1 Chronicles 29:11–12)

Did I not tell you that if you believed you would see the glory of God? (John 11:40)

Other assurance from the Bible: _____

_____

_____ .

When everyone is ready, share some of your responses with the group. What are some of your fears, and what has God said that can help you overcome them?

WRAP-UP AND PRAYER *10 minutes*

As you pray that God would help you to love others more boldly, also pray that he would help you believe his redemptive purposes. Pray that you would see that your kindness to others has a role in his glorious plan—for both them and you.

Lesson

6

GETTING TO WORK

BIG IDEA

We can be sure that our Redeemer will complete his good work in us: he will cover our shame, fill us with his blessings, and turn us into people who love like he does.

BIBLE CONVERSATION *15 minutes*

Where we left off, Boaz promised to redeem Ruth through marriage if another, closer relative to Naomi would not do it. Continue the story by having someone read **Ruth 3:14–18** aloud. Then discuss the questions.

In their nighttime conversation, Ruth asked Boaz to cover her. Although another man is first in line to marry her, how does Boaz begin immediately to cover her in other ways?

At this point in the story, the reader is likely to feel disappointed that it may be someone other than Boaz who will redeem Ruth. Why is that? Why do you feel it's best for Ruth to have Boaz as a husband and not someone else? Why do you feel it's good for Boaz that he be Ruth's redeemer?

Why might it also be good that all involved must be willing to wait and see what God has planned, based on what the other fellow will decide? Why is waiting on God, and letting him decide, often hard for us?

****

The article, "The Business of God," looks especially at Boaz's actions in this passage. Read it aloud, taking turns at the paragraph breaks.

Lesson

ARTICLE

The Business of God

5 minutes

As we resume our journey through this unorthodox romance, we see more and more why Boaz is one of the shining figures in all of biblical history. He appears perfectly committed to trusting the Lord's conditions and reflecting the Lord's character. Boaz is in fact a "type" of Christ—that is to say, though a real historical person, indeed an ancestor of Jesus himself, he is at the same time a symbolic foreshadower of Jesus. I notice three ways that Boaz is like Jesus in this passage.

First, he protects Ruth's reputation. From the previous passage we know that despite having had enough food and wine to become glad, Boaz wasn't inebriated, and he wasn't vulnerable or uninhibited enough to compromise his own integrity. In the morning, in order to protect *Ruth*, lest anyone suspect anything untoward about *her*, he lets her know that he wants her presence to go unknown.

How does this remind you of Jesus? Think of all the times Jesus encountered vulnerable women of checkered backgrounds. The Samaritan woman at the well. The woman of the city with the alabaster jar. In every case, Jesus upheld their dignity, not seeking to exploit their shame but to cover it.

As boss, Boaz is not worried about his reputation. He could likely do what he pleases with anyone he pleases, and there would be little the impoverished or underprivileged could do about it. But Boaz is a man who fears God. Remember that he is a man who does things "as God lives." This means he makes sure that Ruth suffers no shame, just as Christ takes away our shame, covering us by his sacrifice so that the pure image of God in us becomes our reputation.

Second, we see that while Boaz intends to send Ruth home unnoticed, he does not intend to send her home empty-handed. "He said, 'Bring the garment you are wearing and hold it out.' So she held it, and he measured out six measures of barley and put it on her. Then she went into the city."

Boaz owes Ruth nothing. He's already let her further into the fields than she was entitled to go. He's already commanded his workers to look after her. Now he continues to pour from his abundance into her lack. We see that Boaz is exceedingly generous and takes every opportunity to provide.

Isn't Jesus like that? When he feeds five thousand people, there are still twelve baskets left over. When he feeds four thousand, there are seven baskets. When he fills your cup, it runs over. When he gives you affection, he lavishes it. There's always enough of Jesus to be had, and yet always more of him still to have.

When I ponder Boaz's tenderly indulgent care for Ruth, I think of Joel 2:26. "You shall eat in plenty and be satisfied, and praise the name of the LORD your God, who has dealt wondrously with you. And my people shall never again be put to shame." And I think of Jesus who gives living water that eternally satisfies our thirst, who is himself the bread of life that eternally satisfies our hunger.

When you come to Jesus with the empty hand of faith—like perhaps you are this very moment, reading this Bible study for your devotional or spiritual enrichment—he will not send you away without a gift. Like Ruth, then, we come to the feet of our true and better Boaz, Jesus Christ, and we humbly, submissively, vulnerably ask for him to cover us. And the Christ of glory doesn't simply cover us, he crowns us.

Third, Boaz finishes the job. Note Naomi's confidence in Boaz at the end of our passage. "The man will not rest but will settle the matter today." What do we know about Boaz? He's a man of his word. He "handles business." He's going to do whatever it takes to make sure Ruth and Naomi are secure and provided for, so they can finally, perhaps the first time in their lives, *rest*.

And isn't this like Jesus? Isn't Christ's commitment made in perpetuity, without sluggishness or slacking? Even as a child, when his parents came looking for him, he said, "Did you not know that I must be about My Father's business?" (Luke 2:49 NKJV).

Yes, Boaz the go-getting businessman is a reflection of the business-handling Lord of the universe. Don't you think Jesus knows how to handle his business? "And this is the will of him who sent me, that I should lose nothing of all that he has given me, but raise it up on the last day" (John 6:39). Nothing and nobody slips through the cracks. There are no loopholes, aster-isks, exemptions, or expirations on Christ's command of all that he oversees. "He is able to save to the uttermost those who draw near to God through him, since he always lives to make intercession for them" (Hebrews 7:25).

Jesus's life and death and resurrection and glorification are spent in the magnification of God through the rescuing and elevating of his children. Jesus is the guy who does his job! Everybody else is the other guy.

Boaz the "worthy man" will not rest until his efforts are done. And the God-Man who has finished the job of atonement, and who has sent the Holy Spirit to apply it, will not rest until all God's work in you is done. He's settling matters today, right now, this very second, all around the world, and in your very room.

"How are things gonna go?" Naomi basically asks when Ruth gets home. They trust Boaz to see it through to the end. Let's you and I together trust our almighty King Jesus to graciously restore our dignity, abundantly provide for our needs, and eternally perfect the work that he's already begun in us. Jesus perfectly takes care of his business, and *you* are his business.

DISCUSSION *15 minutes*

The article said Jesus's desire is not to point out your shame but to cover it. Do you think of him that way? How is it helpful to do so?

Think of times you come to Jesus—praying, worshiping, read-ing the Bible, or attending this study. Do you expect him to send you home full, with a gift? What difference does that kind of expectation make?

Trusting Jesus to finish his job *in you* means trusting him to grow you in godliness and fit you for heaven. How well do you do this? How could you trust him better?

Lesson

EXERCISE

Worldly Love
and Godly Love

15 minutes

In both this lesson and the previous one, we saw that Ruth and Boaz's nighttime encounter was about a deeper kind of love than we might have expected when we first saw Ruth lie down. Their night was chaste not so much because they avoided tempting situations, but because they had the sort of love that is a reflection of God's perfect love—very different from what the world sometimes calls "love."

If you wish you could love that way, the good news is that you can! Romans 5:5 says, "God's love has been poured into our hearts through the Holy Spirit who has been given to us."

On your own, read through the descriptions of what the world calls love compared to true, godly love. Select several that challenge you or make you hope to love better, and mark these. Also fill in the blank near the bottom of the exercise. Then, as a group, discuss the questions that follow.

WORLDLY "LOVE"...	GODLY LOVE...
...is selective. I prefer to love people who are lovable.	**...is broad.** I love all kinds of people, even those who are hard to love.
...is self-serving. I care more about what I can get from a relationship than what I can give.	**...is sacrificial.** I focus on what I can give, knowing that love is costly—and that's what makes it glorious.
...is reciprocal. I only love those who will love me back.	**...does not expect repayment.** I seek to love my enemies as well as my friends.
...is temporary. I only love as long as I still feel love.	**...is lasting.** I love until I die—and then I keep loving in the next life.
...seeks worldly happiness. I try to make the other person happy in this life.	**...seeks eternal happiness.** I care about the person's spiritual growth and eternal joy.
...is fearful. I worry about what might happen to me, so I hold back.	**...is bold.** It's not all about me, so there's no holding back.
...is fickle. My commitment may change if I, or you, or circumstances change.	**...is dependable.** Much is sure to change, but my love is constant.
...may be detached. I go through the motions of love without really connecting to the person.	**...is personal.** I come near, get involved, and personally bear another's burdens.
...depends on me. If I can't find it in myself to be loving, the love won't happen.	**...depends on God.** The Spirit in me is teaching me to love, and I draw on his power—because love is hard.

WORLDLY "LOVE"...	GODLY LOVE...
...is envious. I am always looking for a better relationship or one like my neighbor has.	**...is content.** Comparing our love to that of others is not the point.
...is partial. I care about the part of the person I find pleasing.	**...is holistic.** I care about the entire person.
...comes from me. I make the rules about how I love based on what I find works for me.	**...comes from God.** I look to God to learn how to love.
...is for me. It brings me honor or a thrill to be part of "the glory of love."	**...is for God.** I love because it brings God honor and glory.
Other: _____ _____ _____	**Other:** _____ _____ _____

The Bible says we love others because God first loved us (1 John 4:19). So now, pick one of your selections and match it with what you know about the life of Jesus. Give an example of how Jesus loved in exactly that way.

Jesus loved this way when he _____

_____

_____ .

When everyone is ready, share some of your findings with the group. What are some ways you hope to grow in godly love? Why are these important to you?

How does Jesus's example, and his similar love for you, help you?

WRAP-UP AND PRAYER *10 minutes*

It's appropriate that the focus of your prayer time together be the struggle to know and practice love. You might

- Pray that God would help you to know his love more deeply.
- Pray that God would show you specific people to love and teach you ways to love them.
- Pray that God would give you the power to love not as the world loves, but as he loves.
- Pray about a specific relationship in your life where you are struggling to love.
- Pray for specific needs of others (this is a way to practice love).

Lesson

7

PROMISES COMING TRUE

BIG IDEA

Our salvation, accomplished by the only true Redeemer, has a glorious end and purpose: it makes great the name of God.

BIBLE CONVERSATION *15 minutes*

Remember that Boaz is going to speak with another potential, first-in-line redeemer and see if that fellow will marry Ruth. In that culture, a relative (usually a brother, but in this case there is none) of a man who had died might agree to take on the man's family and land in the man's name. This would provide for the family and give the dead man—but not the redeemer—an inheritance. Have someone read **Ruth 4:1–10** aloud, and then discuss the questions.

How is Boaz shrewd in the way he conducts the negotiation? What might his tactic reveal about his goals for the negotiation?

What do you think of the first-in-line redeemer's reason for saying no? How common and sensible is his reasoning?

Compare the first-in-line redeemer's reason with Boaz's explanation of why he *will* be the redeemer, found in verses 9 and 10. What are some ways Boaz's reasoning is different? Include reasons not stated but implied.

Which type of reasons do you tend to consider when making decisions, big or small, in your life? Explain.

∗∗∗∗

Read the article aloud now, taking turns at the paragraph breaks.

Redeemed to Perpetuate the Name

5 minutes

Ruth has everything stacked against her. Circumstantially, she is poor and widowed. Her only companion is another woman—who is also poor and widowed. This is not an ideal arrangement for getting ahead in life, especially if you live against the backdrop of the time of the Judges, when people simply did whatever seemed right to them.

Ruth wants to be married. In her sights is an Israelite of noble character and abundant means. In his sights is this foreign woman—considered unclean religiously and ethnically. As a Moabite, she is a descendant of a line begun by incest. If you were looking for the cream of the genetic and cultural crop, you would not start with her.

And yet, the Lord has a surprising and scandalous way of weaving his plans together. Out of a hopeless pile of broken dreams and shattered reputations, there comes a glimmer of light reflecting his glory. He did make humans, the crown of creation, out of dirt after all.

But there are some hiccups in the narrative. What's a good romance without a little conflict? This is the point in the movie where we wonder if the guy and girl will actually end up together. Everything seemed to be going great, until something interrupts the plans. Some challenge or obstacle stands in their way. Will true love prevail?

If it does, it will have to overcome the will of a third party and the legal restrictions of the customs of that day. Remember there is another who is first line for the role of kinsman redeemer, one before Boaz. So our hero goes to speak with him, to discern his intentions. "Then he said to the redeemer, 'Naomi, who has come back from the country of Moab, is selling the parcel of land that belonged to our relative Elimelech'" (v. 3).

Now, at first you may be thinking, *Wait—Naomi's a landowner?* Well, not exactly. Her late husband Elimelech was a landowner. And his plot was part of the common field, which she has no money to work anyway. So Boaz lets this fellow know the rough outline of the matter: there's land available to the family, and you got first dibs.

And of course, the guy wants it. It sounds like a deal to him. But there's a catch: "Boaz said, 'The day you buy the field from the hand of Naomi, you also acquire Ruth the Moabite, the widow of the dead, in order to perpetuate the name of the dead in his inheritance.'" The land and Ruth are a package deal.

The point here is to perpetuate the name of Elimelech, basically by providing a son for Ruth. That son would by custom be the son of Mahlon (her late husband), and the field would be his, technically speaking. Suddenly the deal doesn't look so appealing. *I get land, but I don't really get it,* this guy is probably thinking. *And in order to get this land I don't really get, I have to marry a Moabite woman and have a kid with her who will by custom not really be my son but some dead guy's.*

The guy passes on the deal. Why? Did he not want a wife? Did he not have the money? Did he not want to leave a field to a son who would be considered the son of another man? We don't know. All we know is that when the odds for a Boaz-Ruth love story seem small, there is a surge of hope once again.

And here we have a glimpse of the glory of grace as it is contrasted with the glory of the law. The law is represented by the first kinsman's duty to Ruth. That law is glorious—it is right and true and good. But it cannot redeem. The law does not provide the kinsman with the necessary desire. By God's design, it is grace that saves. Boaz steps up and takes Ruth under his wing. And thus the law only goes so far, while grace redeems fully.

So it is with our redemption. Every other would-be rescuer, any self-effort or agenda for righteousness, only ends up saying along with the first kinsman, "I cannot do it." The idea that there might be multiple redeemer options is a false trail in the story. Christ alone does everything needed to secure our salvation, including paying a great cost himself.

The kinsman first in line takes off his sandal, according to this weird custom scholars aren't quite sure what to make of, and gives it to Boaz, symbolically passing the right to the land—and Ruth—to the next in line. Then Boaz says to everyone there, "You are witnesses this day that I have bought from the hand of Naomi all that belonged to Elimelech and all that belonged to

Chilion and to Mahlon. Also Ruth the Moabite, the widow of Mahlon, I have bought to be my wife, to perpetuate the name of the dead in his inheritance, that the name of the dead may not be cut off from among his brothers and from the gate of his native place" (vv. 9–10).

What a glorious scene! And more evidence of Boaz's noble and selfless character—he will take on this responsibility to perpetuate not his own name but also the names of Elimelech, Mahlon, and Chilion.

And while we're listing the names of all these major characters, we might as well include the kinsman first in line. His name was . . . um, well . . . the text doesn't say. It names the dead guys who aren't even in the story. But do you know the name of the kinsman redeemer first in line?

Exactly. Boaz called him "friend," and the Hebrew behind that word roughly translates as "so-and-so." Whether his reasons for passing on Ruth were good or bad, old So-and-So's name is not perpetuated. But we know who Elimelech, Mahlon, Naomi, and Ruth are because Boaz honored them by honoring God.

And because Boaz honored them by honoring God, his own name is perpetuated, and his son's, and his son's son, and his son's son's son, and so on until the lot of them spill into Matthew 1 and become names in the genealogy of Jesus. That's right, Boaz has redeemed Naomi's plot of land and Ruth's widowed hand in order to perpetuate the name of God's Son, the world's Savior.

And this is why any of us are redeemed: not just so that we'd be personally forgiven and fulfilled, but so that God's name and Christ's lordship would be magnified in every nook and cranny of our lives, spreading into every square inch of the world until we spill into the life and world to come. We are redeemed for his name's sake and to perpetuate his name. "For my name will be great among the nations, says the LORD of hosts" (Malachi 1:11).

DISCUSSION *10 minutes*

What would-be redeemer substitutes for Jesus do people today trust to make life work? Which of them are you tempted to trust?

How does it change you to realize that God is making his name great among the nations, and you are part of the plan?

Go, Tell, Give, Care

20 minutes

The no-name kinsman used the popular "it might cost too much or hurt my family" excuse to get out of helping Ruth and Naomi—and to miss out on a key role in God's redemptive plan. You might think he would have chosen differently had he known the future and been able to see that plan. But he *did* know. He'd surely been told that people like himself, Abraham's descendants, were destined to bless the whole world (see Genesis 22:18). He just couldn't see the details, so he chose not to act that out.

Many life-of-faith choices are like that. Without knowing the details, we must believe God is working salvation and making his name great. God says our acts of faithfulness to him will "be found to result in praise and glory and honor at the revelation of Jesus Christ" (1 Peter 1:7). He says some evildoers will see our actions and respond, becoming people who "glorify God on the day of visitation" (1 Peter 2:12).

For this exercise, think about how that role you have in God's redemptive plan (even though you can't see the details) might encourage you to GO, to TELL, to GIVE, and to CARE.

Read the prompts below and fill in some of the blanks. **You don't have to fill in every blank**—just some where the prompt gives you an idea. Then when everyone is ready, discuss the questions at the end of the exercise.

GO

Going may mean crossing the world or crossing the street. Whichever it is, going to others who need help is a way to follow Jesus, who came to us when we were helpless.

I might go to _____

_____ .

I might help by _____

_____ .

Going excites me because _____

_____ .

Going scares me because _____

_____ .

TELL

Telling can be done in great stadiums or around the breakfast table. It can be formal evangelism or just an encouraging reminder of God. All of this fits people who "proclaim the excellencies of him who called you out of darkness into his marvelous light" (1 Peter 2:9).

I might talk to _____

_____ .

I might tell about _____

_____ .

Telling excites me because _____

_____ .

Telling scares me because _____

_____ .

GIVE

Giving is a tangible way to love others the way Christ loved us, especially when our giving is truly sacrificial.

I might give to _____

_____ .

I might give them _____

_____ .

Giving excites me because _____

_____ .

Giving scares me because _____

_____ .

CARE

Often, just having someone care and be there emotionally, like Jesus was constantly, is a great encouragement. Simply noticing other people, showing interest in them, and finding out about their lives and their needs are the first steps in loving them.

I might show an interest in _____

_____ .

I might ask them about _____

_____ .

Caring excites me because _____

_____ .

Caring scares me because _____

_____ .

Share some of your results with the group. How does the example of Boaz and Ruth encourage you?

What will it take for your excitement to become stronger than your fears, even if you can't fully see how God is working?

WRAP-UP AND PRAYER *10 minutes*

Pray that God would help you live out Jesus's instruction in Matthew 6:19–21. He said, "Do not lay up for yourselves treasures on earth, where moth and rust destroy and where thieves break in and steal, but lay up for yourselves treasures in heaven, where neither moth nor rust destroys and where thieves do not break in and steal. For where your treasure is, there your heart will be also."

- Pray that, unlike the unnamed kinsman, your eyes would be on heavenly treasure and not on your worldly wealth.
- Pray that your heart would follow your heavenly treasure, making you glad to love others.
- Thank God that he redeemed you, and for the unseen but sure treasures that result from living for him.

Lesson

8

IT ENDS WITH
A WEDDING

BIG IDEA

Christ's power at work in us is able to do far more than all we
might ask or imagine.

BIBLE CONVERSATION *20 minutes*

With the way clear for Boaz to marry Ruth, the couple's story
wraps up with rejoicing and a look at Boaz's family history. It
turns out he's descended from Tamar, whose story has simi-
larities to Ruth's in that she too was a foreigner in need of a
redeemer—a role fulfilled by the patriarch Judah, though in his
case he had to be seduced into it (see Genesis 38). There's also
an intriguing look forward in the family line. Have someone
read **Ruth 4:11–22** aloud. Then discuss the questions below.

> Remember that when Naomi first returned to
> Bethlehem, she told the women of the town, "The
> Almighty has dealt very bitterly with me. I went
> away full, and the LORD has brought me back

empty" (Ruth 1:20–21). How has the picture been reversed now? Think of many ways.

The narrator ends by telling a part of the reversal story Naomi, Ruth, and Boaz never knew about in this life: their union leads to David, the great king all Israel needed. Why is it good news that God's story line for our lives includes blessing others?

Why is it good news that God's best and most surprising blessings to us come after we die?

There's a part of the story even the narrator of Ruth didn't see. Have someone read aloud the expanded version of Ruth and Boaz's family line in **Matthew 1:1–16**. Then discuss the final question below.

Imagine the elders and women of Bethlehem had known what Matthew would write centuries later. What might they have added to their statements of blessing and praise? Or what might Naomi, Boaz, or Ruth have proclaimed?

✳✳✳✳

Now take turns reading aloud through the article, and discuss the questions that follow.

Lesson

ARTICLE

The Romance of Redemption

5 minutes

"Boaz took Ruth, and she became his wife. And he went in to her, and the LORD gave her conception, and she bore a son" (Ruth 4:13). Yes, the story of Ruth is a love story. But not the way you might think. The plot begins with the loving commitment between Naomi and Ruth. It continues through the loving commitment between Ruth and Boaz. But the real beginning—and the true end—is in God's love for his children.

There is a lot going on in this little book, more than the eyes can see. Certainly more than Ruth's and Boaz's eyes could see, at least from the vantage point of their immediate circumstances. God had something extraordinarily wonderful planned for this unlikely romance. God had something plotted in his mind from eternity past stretching into eternity future, and that plotline must run straight through this old Jewish man marrying this young Moabite woman in the middle of a land fraught with violence and perversion.

The good news is that the Lord has a way of making a way where there is no way. That the Lord gave Ruth conception with Boaz is to imply she did not have it with Mahlon. I wonder if she ever wondered why she could not bear children with her previous husband. She probably could not foresee then that God meant to do anything redemptive through that situation. Maybe she thought her life would always be that way—that she would be barren forever. When her husband died, I suspect the temptation to doubt the care of God especially kicked in.

The image of Naomi holding the child on her lap and becoming his nurse is exceedingly beautiful. The book began with Naomi as a burdened, bitter woman. She felt completely undone and without hope. I picture tears on her cheeks as she ponders those dark days while her grandson coos and claps his little baby-fatted fists together under her beaming smile.

The women say to Naomi, "Blessed be the LORD, who has not left you this day without a redeemer, and may his name be renowned in Israel!" (v. 15). They don't even know how right they are. The narrator does, however. Because this little baby's name is Obed. And Obed just happens to grow up to father a son named Jesse. And Jesse just happens to grow up to father a son named David.

And of course, none of this "just happens." It is the Storyteller's grand vision all along: an unlikely romance in Bethlehem, which produces a lineage that leads to David, whose kingdom and own lineage makes a providential beeline to the Son of David, the one true King of Israel and the world, Jesus the Messiah.

Trace the line. If you think the inclusion of a poor, widowed Moabite in Jesus's genealogy is scandalous, consider Boaz's own ancestor, Tamar, who through trickery seduced Judah. But you don't have to go that far back to get to the scandal. Boaz's own mother was Rahab, six times referred to as a prostitute in the Scriptures. But this prostitute was redeemed. She too was redeemed to perpetuate the name. The name of Boaz. And the name of Jesus.

Keep going in that genealogy in Matthew. We have Tamar the seductress, Rahab the whore, Ruth the Moabite, Bathsheba the exploited victim of King David's lust. What's remarkable, first, is that women are included in Jesus's genealogy at all! This is outside the Jewish custom, but Matthew includes them. And not just any women, but women with a past, women with a stigma, women with "questions" hanging over them—and men of blatant sin right alongside some of them.

And just as Judges is in the background of Ruth, and just as there is some sordid history in the ancestral background of Ruth and Boaz, the sins we tend to deem dirtier than all others sit there in the background of the Christmas story.

Do you know what this means? It means there is no sin so great that God cannot forgive, and there is no brokenness so big that God cannot redeem. There is no sinner, no failure, no victim, no outsider so far gone that the sovereign hand of the Lord cannot reach and rescue and even revise the story of their life. Jesus's genealogy shows us that God can redeem *anyone*.

But tracing Ruth and Boaz's strange, quirky relationship all the way to the Messiah also reminds us that while the Lord is writing our story, we ought not to forget *he's* the real star!

Spiritually speaking, we're all poor, widowed Moabites. We have nothing to offer God. We have no hope in human capital for our own redemption. Religiously, spiritually, we are unclean and unworthy. And yet the Lord in his kindness comes to dignify sinners like us. He provides his own flesh and blood by dying on the cross to atone for our sins. We fall to the forces of wickedness and conspire with them, but he conquers them. He satisfies the wrath of God, and we are united to him in a strange, unlikely marriage of eternal perpetuity. Why? That the riches of his grace might be known and magnified.

Like Ruth, we cannot manage this with what we've got. We cannot pull ourselves up by our bootstraps. We don't have what it takes. Even if we white-knuckled our way to obedience, we couldn't climb out of the hole of unrighteousness we find ourselves in. The law? He is the first kinsman. He says, "I cannot redeem you." The true and better kinsman redeemer is Christ. He says, "See, I have won the hand of my church."

This is good news, friend. Whatever you're clinging to that's holding you back from Christ, you can let go. He will hold you fast. Whatever you're falling prey to, you can conquer. He will strengthen you. Whatever you're engaging in that is not of God, you can repent of it. His grace is sufficient. We are redeemed (thank God!) to perpetuate his name (praise God!).

DISCUSSION *10 minutes*

Where to do sense you might be today in the larger story God is writing with your life? (If you think your study of Ruth has moved that story along, explain how.)

What are you clinging to that's holding you back from Christ? Or what are you falling prey to that you need his strength to conquer?

Lesson

EXERCICE

8

Blessings in Ruth

15 minutes

In the course of these lessons, you may have noticed that much of the dialogue in the book of Ruth is spoken in the form of blessings. These blessings convey many of the book's key messages for us, its readers.

For this exercise, look back on five of the blessings in Ruth, which are printed below. Read each blessing and consider what it means to you (remembering that the husband/redeemer in this story turns out to be a picture of Jesus, and Israel is God's people). Then answer for yourself the three questions at the end of the exercise. You'll finish by sharing your responses with the group.

> Naomi to her daughters-in-law:
> "The LORD grant that you may find rest, each of you in the house of her husband!" (Ruth 1:9)

> Boaz to Ruth:
> "A full reward be given you by the LORD, the God of Israel, under whose wings you have come to take refuge!" (2:12)

Naomi about Boaz:
"May he be blessed by the LORD, whose kindness has not forsaken the living or the dead!" (2:20)

The town elders to Boaz:
"May the LORD make the woman, who is coming into your house, like Rachel and Leah, who together built up the house of Israel. May you act worthily in Ephrathah and be renowned in Bethlehem." (4:11)

The women to Naomi:
"Blessed be the LORD, who has not left you this day without a redeemer, and may his name be renowned in Israel! He shall be to you a restorer of life." (4:14)

QUESTIONS:

Which blessing would you say best sums up the main message of the book of Ruth, and why?

Which blessing best conveys how this study has been meaningful to you personally, and why?

Which blessing would you most like to have someone speak about you, and why?

When everyone is ready, share your results with the group.

WRAP-UP AND PRAYER *10 minutes*

Continue to ask your Father for all that you need—for more, even, than you can imagine! You may want to use some of the blessings in Ruth as a model for your prayers for each other.

LEADER'S NOTES

These notes provide some thoughts on the study's discussion questions and exercises, especially the Bible conversation sections, mostly from the editor who composed those questions. The discussion leader should read these notes before the study begins. Occasionally, the leader may want to refer the group to a point found here.

However, it is important that you NOT treat these notes as a way to look up the "right answer." In most cases, the best answers will be those the group discovers *on its own* through reading and thinking about the Bible passages and articles. You will lose the value of looking closely at what the Bible says, and taking time to think about it, if you are too quick to turn to these notes.

LESSON 1: EVERYTHING FALLS APART

The list of ways Naomi's life fell apart and the potential problems she worries about is long. When her family first moved to Moab, Naomi likely lost the support of extended relatives and her faith community. When her husband and sons died, those losses became still greater and were combined with the loss of dearly loved ones.

In that time and place, Naomi probably also lost much of her economic security, since she was without male family members to provide for her. Her social standing and legacy would also be compromised, even if she returned to Bethlehem. Without children, how could she contribute to society or make any lasting impact? She was doomed to be miserable, irrelevant, and forgotten.

Naomi might find several places to lay blame. She could blame her husband or herself for the decisions to move to Moab, to stay there, and to let their sons marry Moabite women. She might think she was suffering the consequences of bad decisions, or divine punishment for bad faith. She also might have found others to blame: the book of Judges shows that the whole community of Israel often brought calamity like famine upon themselves by forsaking the Lord, and Israel's weak leaders certainly share blame for many of the nation's troubles.

But Naomi prefers to pin the responsibility on God. This may sound opposed to God, but actually there is wisdom and faith in it. God can handle the responsibility for tragedy. Naomi seems to see, correctly, that God is in control of all things—even people's mistakes and sins—and he uses them to accomplish his goals. If she were in control, she would return to Bethlehem determined to do better this time. But God-in-control means she will return intending to live by faith.

Though it seems Naomi can't envision how, by attributing her calamity to almighty God she might be acknowledging that he can also reverse it. Still, her claim in verse 13 that the Lord's hand is "against" her suggests that, like many of us, she struggles to believe God's plan for her is anything but unhappy. It will take the rest of the book for her to understand that she is wrong, and even then she won't see the half of it.

LESSON 2: THE BLESSING IN THE BITTER END

Ruth's pledge of commitment to Naomi is one of the strongest pledges recorded anywhere in the Bible. It is a lifelong commitment that lasts even into the grave, and it includes all aspects of Ruth's life: her decision-making, her lifestyle, her relationships, and her spirituality. Even our closet human commitments seldom go this far. They usually come with an "out clause," or involve mutual promises. Ruth foregoes all of this; her pledge has no limits.

It is also one of the greatest professions of faith anywhere in the Bible. Ruth puts herself under the care of the true God with no backup plan, no encouraging community, and little expectation that anything but hard times are ahead. God has made her no promises of worldly happiness, and based on Naomi's experiences Ruth has no reason to expect any. Yet she comes to God anyway, empty, giving only herself and gaining only him. She is willing to share Naomi's bitter life so that, under no protection but the Lord's, she can be of help to her mother-in-law.

As for Naomi, there's a difference between a complaint against God that also rejects him and his authority, and a lament that cries to God for answers in hard times but remains faithful. Naomi's behavior in this story suggests that despite her complaining, she still has faith. In fact, her faith may be all the more impressive because there's nothing fancy or pretend about it and it has persevered through the worst. And we probably should not be too hard on her for failing to notice God's mercies. His good plans are often hard to discern, especially when we are hurting.

LESSON 3: THINGS TAKE A TURN

A close look at Boaz's interactions when he arrives at his field reveals an interest in God and in others. He does not inquire about how the work is going or what progress has been made, but seems concerned for his workers as people rather than merely as employees who can serve his purposes. He wants them to know the Lord's blessing. He is also interested in Ruth, the new gleaner is his field, not because he wants to know if she has stayed out of the way and behaved herself, but because he's interested in her personal story and family background. Again, his concern for others comes before his concern for his business.

Unlike some men, Boaz does not seem to be evaluating Ruth on her looks, or her charm, or how she might be able to satisfy him, but rather on her character. And unlike some managers, he doesn't assess her in terms of value and liabilities, but rather by how his farm can support her godly flourishing.

It is likely that the Rahab mentioned in Matthew 1:5 as the mother of Boaz is the same Rahab who hid the Israelite spies when God was preparing to bring his people into the promised land, else why would Matthew mention her? She was not necessarily the direct mother of Boaz, since Matthew appears to skip generations in his genealogy of Jesus (mentioning only the highlights) and the events in Ruth seen to have taken place well after the conquest of the land. The number of places Rahab is commended in Scripture after her initial mention (Joshua 6:23ff, Hebrews 11:31, James 2:25) suggests she was remembered, and that Boaz would have been aware of his special heritage. A person who knows he belongs to a bunch of former outsiders brought near to God—and this is all of us—should be attuned to welcoming other outsiders.

As the introduction to this study mentioned, the picture of faith that imagines Ruth taking refuge under the wings of the Lord is repeated in five of the psalms of her descendant, David (Psalms 17:8; 36:7; 57:1; 61:4; 63:7). It is also used by her more distant descendant, Jesus, when he describes the faith he wishes the people of Jerusalem would have in him (see Matthew 23:37). This makes refuge under the wings of the Lord one of the Bible's chief images of faith. Boaz's blessing acknowledges Ruth's faith and implies a wish that it would continue and grow—a sweet blessing indeed!

DISCUSSION: It may seem counterintuitive that not having to prove our religious output can actually improve our devotion to God. But if we did have to prove our worth to God, our failure would be utterly discouraging and our motive for obedience would be selfish—which would only add yet another moral failure. When we serve God instead as a response to his friendly grace, we obey with more powerful and purer motives: love, gratitude, hope in his promises, and excited confidence in his work in us, to name just a few.

EXERCISE: Receiving grace and giving grace are so inter-twined in the Christian life that it is a mistake to try to separate them. Receiving grace is such a transformative experience that it will compel us to love others, and loving others is such a God-dependent task that it will compel us to seek more of his grace.

LESSON 4: THINGS ARE LOOKING UP

NOTE: The leader should not let the Bible conversation move on after just a few observations about Ruth's life-changing day. There are many changes to see, and patience should allow the group to make several observations that might otherwise be missed.

Ruth experiences one unexpected blessing after another on her first day in Boaz's field. She had probably arrived merely hoping to be able to glean in a place where she was tolerated. Instead, Boaz welcomes her with admiration and invites her to share his table. She is brought into his workplace family, so to speak. She is well on her way to making friends and being established in the community, despite Naomi's predictions back in Moab. She is also well-fed. For the first time in this story we read of someone having more than enough.

By afternoon, it becomes obvious that her time as a barely-surviving gleaner is already over. She is able to see that she and Naomi will eat amply, not sparingly. She also has respect and protection. As she struggles to carry home her day's gatherings, the realization of the kindness she received must be as staggering as her load.

The end of the day reveals still more. There is a promise of continued abundance, safety, and friendship throughout the harvest. It is one thing to eat for a day, another to have the comfort of knowing you will eat for the foreseeable future. More than that, Naomi and Ruth have a family member who is eager to show them kindness and may be willing to act as their long-term protector and redeemer—one to take them into his family after the deaths of their husbands. This development brings hope and joy to a household that had been fixated on bitterness. Perhaps best of all, it brings the realization that the Lord is kind to them after all.

In this section Boaz becomes even more clearly a pattern for Christ, his descendant who was to come later. Jesus loves to prepare a table for his people and eat with them. He provides life-giving blessings in abundance. This lesson's article and exercise go into more detail.

LESSON 5: THE PLOT THICKENS

Despite the possibility of some sexual overtones in this passage, a close look gives us reason to believe something else—something much deeper—is actually at play here. Remember that Ruth is following Naomi's instructions, and Naomi has not told her to seduce or "lie with him," as the Bible typically speaks of sexual intercourse. She even begins her instructions showing her desire that Ruth find rest and care, so it does not seem likely that she intends for Ruth to put herself in a compromising position. Perhaps this is even some custom of the time, a way for women to safely identify to would-be suitors their availability. On Ruth's behalf, there could be a level of naiveté. She has not only her loyalty to Naomi inclining her to follow Naomi's instructions, but also her relative newness to the faith and her foreignness to the country. If this is not how matches are made in Judah, she might not know it.

But we have other reasons to doubt anything untoward is intended. For one, the scene takes place at the threshing floor where Boaz, and likely several others, has been working. It seems probable that there would be others in the immediate area. Secondly, the Bible doesn't tend to blanch at anyone's sinfulness, including protagonists in covenantal history. If Ruth seduced Boaz sexually, we should expect the text to say it rather plainly.

Thirdly, and perhaps most importantly, sexual impropriety simply doesn't fit what we know about Boaz and Ruth so far. From all the clues we get to their character in the rest of the story, a premarital seduction is not what they're after. In fact, the passage commends Ruth for *not* selfishly looking for a young guy who promises sexual excitement or will stroke her ego by being seen as a great catch. Ruth seeks godliness and growth in the Lord's favor, a guy who will spread his garment of the Redeemer's love over her, and she is thinking of Boaz and Naomi ahead of her "needs." Likewise, Boaz desires to love Ruth's whole person the way God does—not just take her body—and is even willing to let another fellow do it if that guy can prove worthy. He too is thinking of others first.

As a result, the image of Ruth spending the night at Boaz's feet is not one of impropriety, but security. She is safe there. She has come to a strange land and found rest.

Had this situation played out among two people whose eyes were not firmly on God's redemption, it may indeed have progressed sinfully. Matthew Henry comments, "Few could have come so near the fire as they did and not have been scorched."[3] But Ruth's and Boaz's godly characters, with their eyes set on God's grace, makes all the difference. We do well to avoid tempting situations, but above all we need our eyes on Jesus.

As for Ruth's boldness, she is even more fearless in her interaction with Boaz than Naomi had counselled. Naomi said Boaz would tell her what to do, but Ruth leaves no doubts about her intentions as she tells Boaz what to do. It's clear she is inviting him to marry her. Boaz's actions so far in this story should have given her some confidence that he would do as she asked. It's easy to ask a man of godly character to do a godly thing, even if it is a hard thing to ask. But beyond this, we have seen that Ruth has faith in God. It was her desire to live under God's caring wings that brought her to Bethlehem in the first place, and with her trust in his provision that sent her out to glean. Here again she has faith that pursuing a godly goal (marriage to

---

3. Matthew Henry, *Commentary on the Whole Bible* (McLean, VA: MacDonald), 2:270.

a faithful man) is the right course of action—regardless of how risky or awkward it may feel. Her choice is to do what's right and loving, even if it's hard. She understands that "the upright will inhabit the land, and those with integrity will remain in it" (Proverbs 2:21).

Ruth uses covenantal language that hints at God's care for his people. She is not merely asking Boaz to marry her; she is asking him to be a godly husband. She appeals to him to be an instrument of God's care for her. She invites him to love her as Christ loved the church, sacrificing in order to redeem her. As a man eager to practice godliness, Boaz jumps at so rich an offer.

LESSON 6: GETTING TO WORK

Boaz lets Ruth know immediately that he is acting like her redeemer, even though it's possible he won't ultimately be her redeemer. He has already invited her to spend the night safely at his feet. He has promised to see to her request immediately, "in the morning." Now he also safeguards her reputation by having her leave before full light (not because they have done anything shameful, but lest anyone else suspect it of her). And he sends her away with a generous gift, perhaps as a tangible assurance that he is ready to be her redeemer or even as a token similar to what one might give a bride-to-be, if the engagement were official.

Neither Ruth nor Boaz seems to feel any shame over her poverty or gleaning, or her Moabite heritage. But when it comes to her spending the night with him, they are careful not only to act appropriately but also to make sure Ruth suffers no shame due to any misunderstanding or unkind gossip about them. They share a godly sense of what would be shameful if it were true, and what is true but not shameful.

Boaz and Ruth share a desire for godliness and an urge to be part of God's redeeming purposes. It truly is beautiful to observe their particular kind of love. They are soul mates—in the best, Christian sense of the word. They both seem to understand that Ruth's soul has experienced the welcome and generosity of God through Boaz, and that Boaz's heart has been stirred to love sacrificially by caring for Ruth.

DISCUSSION NOTE: You may need to point out that trusting Jesus for our growth in godliness does not mean we are inactive. On the contrary, we work hard at godliness. But it is an effort we undertake *by faith*. This is first of all an internal disposition:

we cry constantly to God, acknowledging that if he does not turn us from sin, nothing will; we believe his promises to us; we rely on his Spirit in us. But the exercise of this faith can also be seen externally: we are diligent in prayer; we depend on God's word both written and preached; we seek the support of Christ's church. These are behaviors that mark a person of faith, and they come alongside any effort in godliness that is truly dependent on God. You may want to refer participants to the "lifestyle of receiving grace" in exercise 3.

LESSON 7: PROMISES COMING TRUE

Like many shrewd negotiators, Boaz does not reveal up front what he wants most from the negotiation. The way he brings up Ruth partway through the discussion shows that he has been angling for her redemption. Once the first-in-line kinsman commits to the deal, Boaz mentions the full responsibilities, forcing the kinsman to either refuse the deal or take on his obligations fully.

By getting the other fellow to say yes at the outset, Boaz might have been giving him every opportunity to see how glorious and godly it would be to redeem Ruth. Or perhaps Boaz was testing the man, finding out if this potential husband for Ruth was truly godly or just interested in himself and money. Maybe Boaz was exposing him publicly so that the Bethlehem community would be supportive when Boaz married Ruth instead. In any case, we can see that the kinsman does not possess the worthiness we want in a husband for Ruth.

When the first-in-line kinsman ducks out of the deal, he explains that he is thinking about his own inheritance. In contrast, Boaz speaks only about the inheritance of others. He speaks of five other people—three of them already dead—who will benefit, without any mention of what is in it for himself. Boaz also mentions the town, suggesting he is concerned that all Bethlehem flourish under God's design for the care of everyone. His opening words in the book of Ruth, "The LORD be with you!" (2:4), are proven to be more than a traditional and pious-sounding greeting. Boaz's instinct truly is to see others as God sees them, and to want them to enjoy God's presence and redemption.

LESSON 8: IT ENDS WITH A WEDDING

Naomi arrived in Bethlehem speaking a lament and very nearly accusing God of not being a good God; now she hears praise for his goodness. She arrived bitter; now she is glad. She arrived expecting no future to speak of; now everyone is speaking of her promising future. She arrived empty; now her arms are full with a child. She arrived speaking of calamity; now she is amazed by the turn of events in her life. She arrived unwilling to hear even a single-word mention of gladness; now she accepts a long blessing. She arrived without any word of appreciation for Ruth; now she realizes the great worth of Ruth's love.

It seemed at the beginning of the book that Naomi might hope to receive some kindness, but that she surely had nothing to give. One of the sweetest parts of the reversal God works in her life is that he makes her a blessing for others. Because of her return, they have seen the commitment of a true redeemer. Because of her, they praise God. Because of her, they will have the good king they need.

The fact that the ripples of this extend even beyond Naomi's life in this world, and include the salvation of many, should encourage us when we struggle to see any good behind our situation. We too have hard times, whether brief disappointments or extended "famines." Sometimes, like Naomi and Ruth, we are able to start seeing before this life is over how God is reversing our sadness—but not always. Even when we do see glimpses, they hardly compare to the glories that will be revealed to us, and in us, one day.

mission
propelled by good news

At Serge we believe that mission begins through the gospel of Jesus Christ bringing God's grace into the lives of believers. This good news also sustains and empowers us to cross nations and cultures to bring the gospel of grace to those whom God is calling to himself.

As a cross-denominational, reformed sending agency with more than two hundred missionaries and twenty-five teams in five continents, we are always looking for people who are ready to take the next step in sharing Christ through:

- **Short-term Teams:** One- to two-week trips oriented around serving overseas ministries while equipping the local church for mission

- **Internships:** Eight-week to nine-month opportunities to learn about missions through serving with our overseas ministry teams

- **Apprenticeships:** Intensive twelve- to twenty-four-month training and ministry opportunities for those discerning their call to cross-cultural ministry

- **Career:** One- to five-year appointments designed to nurture you for a lifetime of ministry

 Grace at the Fray   **Visit us online at: serge.org/mission**

spiritual renewal resources for you

Disciples who are motivated and empowered by grace to reach out to a broken world are handmade, not mass-produced. Serge intentionally grows disciples through curricula, discipleship experiences, and training programs.

Resources for Every Stage of Growth

Serge offers grace-based, gospel-centered studies for every stage of the Christian journey. Every level of our materials focuses on essential aspects of how the Spirit transforms and motivates us through the gospel of Jesus Christ.

- **101**: The Gospel-Centered Series
  Gospel-centered studies on Christian growth, community, work, parenting, and more

- **201**: The Gospel Transformation Series
  These studies go a step deeper into gospel transformation, involve homework and more in-depth Bible study

- **301**: The Sonship Course and Serge Individual Mentoring

Mentored Sonship

For more than twenty-five years Serge has been discipling ministry leaders around the world through our Sonship course to help them experience the freedom and joy of having the gospel transform every part of their lives. A personal discipler will help you apply what you are learning to the daily struggles and situations you face, as well as, model what a gospel-centered faith looks and feels like.

Discipler Training Course

Serge's Discipler Training Course helps you gain biblical understanding and practical wisdom you need to disciple others so they experience substantive, lasting growth in their lives. Available for on-site training or via distance learning, our training programs are ideal for ministry leaders, small group leaders or those seeking to grow in their ability to disciple effectively.

 Grace at the Fray   **Find more resources at serge.org**

resources and mentoring
for every stage of
growth

Every day around the world, Serge teams help people develop and deepen a living, breathing, growing relationship with Jesus. We help people connect with God in ways that are genuinely grace-motivated and increase desire and ability to reach out to others. No matter where you are along the way, we have a series that is right for you.

101: The Gospel-Centered Series

Our *Gospel-Centered* series is simple, deep, and transformative. Each *Gospel-Centered* lesson features an easy-to-read article and provides challenging discussion questions and application questions. Best of all, no outside preparation on the part of the participants is needed! They are perfect for small groups, those who are seeking to develop "gospel DNA" in their organizations and leaders, and contexts where people are still wrestling with what it means to follow Jesus.

201: The Gospel Transformation Series

Our *Gospel Transformation* studies take the themes introduced in our 101-level materials and expand and deepen them. Designed for those seeking to grow through directly studying Scripture, each *Gospel Transformation* lesson helps participants grow in the way they understand and experience God's grace. Ideal for small groups, individuals who are ready for more, and one-on-one mentoring, *Gospel Identity, Gospel Growth,* and *Gospel Love* provide substantive material, in easy-to-use, manageable sized studies.

The Sonship Course and Individual Mentoring from Serge

Developed for use with our own missionaries and used for over twenty-five years with thousands of Christian leaders in every corner of the world, Sonship sets the standard for whole-person, life transformation through the gospel. Designed to be used with a mentor or in groups ready for a high investment with each other, each lesson focuses on the type of "inductive heart study" that brings about change from the inside out.

 Grace at the Fray   **Visit us online at serge.org**

www.newgrowthpress.com